THE STORY OF SUSAN INGOUF LAFFERTY

BARBARA JOINER

Woman's Missionary Union
Birmingham, Alabama

Woman's Missionary Union
P. O. Box 830010
Birmingham, AL 35283-0010

Dewey Decimal Classification: 922.6
   Subject Headings: LAFFERTY, SUSAN INGOUF
                    MISSIONARY BIOGRAPHY
                    MISSIONS—PAKISTAN
                    MISSIONS, INTERNATIONAL

Scripture quotations indicated by CEV are from *Contemporary English Version.* Copyright ©American Bible Society 1991. Used by permission.

   Scripture quotations indicated by NIV are from the Holy Bible, New International Version. Copyright ©1973, 1978, 1984 International Bible Society. Used by permission of Zondervan Bible Publishers.

Cover design by Janell E. Young
Cover illustration and inside illustrations by Jane Chu Thompson

ISBN: 1-56309-234-4
W986103•1198•3M2

Words of Thanksgiving

I thank my husband, Homer, who endured another book (after I promised I'd never do another one)!

I thank my Acteen granddaughter, Megan Vansant, for reading and approving every word!

I thank my other granddaughter, Jacqueline Head, for eating only two pages of the manuscript!

I thank Susan's parents, John and Glenn Ingouf, for checking every single word (and correcting many)!

I thank everyone who sent letters to share words about Susan. You all are wonderful!

I thank my editor, Becky Nelson, for keeping the email hot sending all my messages!

I thank every long-suffering friend for praying me through!

I thank the Lord that I am finished!

Words About Contents

Some Before Words

This is a book about Susan Lafferty who serves with her husband, Todd, in Karachi, Pakistan. It has lots of words—nearly 25,000! The title, *Not Simply with Words,* echoes "words." Every chapter heading shouts "words." However, for many years, Susan was considered someone with few words. Oh, she had plenty of words around her family, around friends. But others saw her quietness, her shyness, her few words. Her words were written in journals, sketched on paper, prayed to the Father. Then she began to write words. She gave her words to the Lord and she performed those words to thrill across the footlights.

In spite of her giftedness with words, Susan continues to live out her chosen Scripture: "My dear friends, God loves you, and we know he has chosen you to be his people. When we told you the good news, it was with the power and assurance that come from the Holy Spirit, and not simply with words. You knew what kind of people we were and how we helped you" (1 Thess. 1:4,5 CEV).

In her journey as a missionaries' kid (MK) in Indonesia, as a student in the United States (US), and now with her family in Pakistan, Susan has lived among us. She has not only talked the talk, she has walked the walk—and brought glory and honor to the Lord Jesus Christ.

1

BEGINNING WORDS IN INDONESIA

Susan Lynn Ingouf was born August 5, 1958, in Hartselle, Alabama, to John and Glenn Ingouf. Her father was pastor of West Hartselle Baptist Church. When Susan was only 2, her parents were appointed Southern Baptist missionaries to the island nation of Indonesia.

For the next 16 years, Susan would call this exotic land home. John and Glenn would continue to serve in Indonesia for 12 more years.

Look at the map on page 99. See all those islands called Indonesia? To give you an idea of their size, take all the states east of the Mississippi River. Chop into 3,000 pieces. Scatter across 3,000 miles of ocean around the equator between Asia and Australia. Instant Indonesia!

The names of some of the islands are familiar. Java is the island where the Ingoufs lived. Sumatra is another big island. Parts of two of the world's largest islands, Borneo and New Guinea, are Indonesian. The tiny island of Bali and thousands of other small islands make up the rest of the largest chain of islands in the world.

Pack on these islands over 206 million people speaking 250 languages and dialects.

On Christmas Day 1951, three Southern Baptist missionaries landed in the capital city of Jakarta. Ten years later little Susan arrived with her parents and a brand-new sister, Ann. The Ingoufs had to wait for visa clearance in Bangkok, Thailand, for eight months. It was in Bangkok that Ann was born.

Glenn, Susan's mom, recalls leaving San Francisco for Indonesia aboard the ship *President Cleveland*. Susan was only 2. Someone asked Glenn, "You're not taking Susan with you, are you?" Not only did Susan go, she went with a song in her heart! She could already sing "Jesus Loves Me" and actually sang it on talent night with the ship's orchestra accompanying her!

The Ingouf family went to Bandung on the island of Java for language study. Then they moved to the port city of Surabaya.

Wilma Weeks, a single missionary who had served in China and India before going to Indonesia, lived next door to the Ingoufs. Aunt Wilma, as the Ingouf children call her, recalls that a small backyard separated her house from theirs. Aunt Wilma's dining room window, always open, faced the little yard. Susan and Ann, and later brother John and sister Julie, played on the swing and in the little plastic pool. They were family.

Susan happily remembers lots of running, playing hard, climbing trees, roller-skating, playing house, and climbing on monkey bars. Later on, she became an avid reader, loved to play pretend, and to draw.

"We had plenty of family time—and typical sibling fights, pinches, and loud arguments," she laughs. "I was the oldest child and rather hardheaded."

Aunt Wilma listened to Susan read her first sentences. From then on, there was no stopping her. She was reading one day after lunch in 1963 and suddenly the room grew dark. Susan turned on the light and then discovered that Gunung Agung, an active volcano on Bali, had erupted! It was pitch dark outside and "dry rain" was falling. Aunt Vandy (missionary Ruth Vanderburg) was visiting

Aunt Wilma, and she called out to them, "I don't know about you—but if the Lord's come back, *we're still here!*"

In those beginning years in Indonesia, the Communists were strong. During the times of unrest, sirens went off to signal blackouts. Every light had to go out. Susan remembers they shut the curtains and put a sock over a flashlight to have a tiny bit of light.

Anti-American feeling was strong. Susan recalls waking up one morning to find anti-American slogans painted all over the front wall at their house—right next to her bedroom window.

"One night I remember being afraid, thinking I could hear something outside that window. Dad took me outside and showed me the moon and stars on a beautiful clear night. He talked about the Lord watching over us. I felt such peace."

Later, during tense times, Susan rode her bike three blocks to the bread store to get some bread. When she returned she told her mom that she'd ridden by some Indonesian girls. Two had spit on her. On her way home, she decided to ride back the same way and smile. They smiled back at her!

Susan already had many Indonesian friends. When she was 5 she had attended an Indonesian kindergarten at a Christian school nearby. Her mother said that she seemed to enjoy it and fit in, although later Susan confided that she was scared because they knew more about arithmetic than she did!

"We heard one day that the whole kindergarten was being vaccinated for smallpox," Glenn said. "They made two huge, long scrapes down the arm to vaccinate. Susan had already been vaccinated, so John raced to the school on his motor scooter to stop it. Too late! Susan was already the proud owner of those two long needle marks!"

When Susan began first grade, her mom taught her. Glenn converted the guest room over the garage into a regular classroom with desks, blackboards, posters, and a science area. Susan remembers that she was allowed to see the covers of the next textbooks when they arrived. "It was a teaser," she laughs. "I anticipated the first day of school so that I could open those books!"

"Mom even rang the school bell," Susan declares. "She made school very interesting."

Aunt Wilma boasts that reading was easy for Susan. "Whenever she finished a primer, she would appear at my front door. We would sit on the sofa and she'd read the book to me. When she advanced to thicker readers, I heard her mother caution her to just choose one favorite story to read to me."

However, Aunt Wilma knew that Susan wanted to read more than one story, so she would ask for more. "She read eagerly and very well, with expression," remembers Aunt Wilma.

All of the Ingouf children read to Aunt Wilma except the youngest, Julie. The Ingoufs were moving to Bandung. Susan sorrowfully announced that Julie would never learn to read because she wouldn't be able to go over and read to Aunt Wilma!

There were always lots of books to read. Lucille Wiggins and Sarah Pickens, sisters and schoolteachers in Hartselle, Alabama, had their schoolchildren pick their favorite books. Then they would send those books to the Ingouf children. Susan remembers those treasures: the Boxcar Children, Nancy Drew mysteries, *Little Women, Heidi,* and all sorts of biographies of famous people.

They also went often to the US Information Service Library until it was closed by Communists in 1964. After that they went to the British Council Library.

Susan also loved to write—beginning in elementary school. At 9 she decided to write a book, and she wrote a short series of children's stories. And always, she wrote poetry. As a seventh-grader, she decided she needed a typewriter. She asked God to help her save for one and promised to dedicate her writing to Him. He did and she did. She bought a very nice typewriter that lasted through high school, college, and most of seminary!

Drawing and sketching was another skill Susan developed. Her mom explains that when they went to the seamstresses (there were no ready-made clothes in Indonesia) even at age 9 Susan would draw what she wanted made. She also drew wonderful maps and made her own Indonesian notecards.

And she was always dramatic. She mimicked everybody. She could do little old grandmas to bobby-soxers. She and her friends did plays and circuses, complete with tickets.

When Susan was 9, Aunt Wilma took her on as one of her piano students. She even gave her a kitchen timer to set for her 30 minutes of daily practice. Glenn claims that Susan practiced when she didn't have to. However, Susan admits that she had a bad habit of moving the timer forward so that she could finish and go out to play!

Aunt Wilma claims not to be a real musician, but is proud she gave Susan her start. She had other teachers later and became an accomplished pianist and now plays for her church in Karachi.

She went to a piano school in Surabaya next, and gave her only piano recital. The governor of East Java and other important people attended! "I was so nervous," Susan admits, "that I went out and played 'Fur Elise' one octave higher than it was supposed to be played!"

Balinese dance lessons, ballet, and swimming lessons gave Susan a well-rounded education.

Beginning words in Indonesia were in English, in Indonesian, and in Javanese. And a lot of those words were about Jesus.

2

WORDS ABOUT JESUS

Susan remembers with joy growing up in a loving home, under the influence of parents who loved the Lord and were seeking to grow in their relationship with Him. "We usually read a devotional or verses aloud each morning at breakfast and prayed together. We also had 'family altar'—coming together once a week for a time of family worship."

So it's no wonder that when Susan was only 3 her mother called her for the fifth time to come shower. Glenn found her undressed, ready for the shower, standing and staring at the wall. She asked, "Susan Lynn Ingouf, what in the world are you thinking about?" Susan replied, "I'm thinking about Jesus."

Several years later, Susan and her mom were talking about God and Susan told her that she liked talking about God. "I wish God was here. Can He breathe? I wish we could see God." She continued,

9

"It's hard to believe. Anyway, if God wasn't here, nothing would be here."

When she was 6, Susan went to her parents' bedroom and asked her mom how to have Jesus in her heart. Glenn explained to her very simply. In 1966, while the Ingoufs were home on furlough, Susan asked her dad to walk down the aisle with her and she made public her decision to accept Jesus as Savior. A short time later, she was baptized at Highland Baptist Church in Shreveport, Louisiana.

In Surabaya, the Ingoufs attended Immanuel Baptist Church. Mrs. Tan, Susan's Sunday School teacher, encouraged her to read aloud in her Indonesian Bible. She loved to do that and often taught the lesson in Indonesian to sister Ann and brother John—if he'd sit still long enough!

Glenn and some other missionary moms had "Monday School" for their children so they could experience English-speaking Bible teaching as well. Also, since John was a church planter, the whole family often went with him in the evenings. They would pack the pump organ and themselves into the van and take off. They met in living rooms, on porches, in an old factory with dirt floors complete with chickens running about.

Most nights they worshiped by kerosene lanterns or pump lights. They often had hot tea in glasses along with some sort of snack. It was never boring.

Glenn had completed all of the Girls' Auxiliary (forerunner to Acteens) Forward Steps (forerunner to StudiAct) and was presented with her cape as Queen Regent. She longed for Susan to be a GA. Aunt Wilma came to the rescue and led a group for Susan and her friends. They began with four girls. However, one by one, they lost members as parents moved away. Finally, only Susan remained.

Susan says, "I well remember studying missions, learning about Paul's missionary journeys, and memorizing Scriptures for GA steps."

She did all the work on Forward Steps through Princess. Then the Ingoufs went home on furlough. However, they reached the US just in time for Susan to be in a coronation service!

One of Susan's favorite activities in Indonesia was going to Camp MiKi. Starting at age 9 Susan went to Camp MiKi for ten days each summer. This camp for missionaries' kids (MKs) was started and conducted by missionary Catherine Walker for many years. Aunt Wilma says that Susan was overjoyed when she reached the magic age to go. They cheered her off and eagerly awaited for her homecoming. After a few days she had Ann and John singing the camp songs and looking forward to their ninth birthdays!

Susan points to Camp MiKi as valuable time with her peers and a real help in her spiritual, emotional, and social growth. "We had Bible studies, arts and crafts, sports, teamwork, chores (KP duty), and special programs in the evening that included campfires or skits or a special banquet. Each year we had a 'candlelight service' towards the end of camp when people shared testimonies," Susan recalls. "This was one of those places where I learned to share what was on my heart."

Before camp began, MKs memorized Scripture and the books of the Bible to prepare for Bible Sword Drills. Susan was greatly challenged and worked really hard.

Accommodations were rustic, but the mountains were beautiful. "I had many 'mountaintop experiences' there," Susan claims.

On her first campout at Camp MiKi, Susan heard a crackling sound. They looked over and saw the red glow of lava flowing down the side of Mount Merapi! Glenn laughs, "One missionary mom mentioned that she hesitated to write to her mother about the thrill of sitting on a ledge of a mountain trail and watching lava cascade down the mountain!"

Another less than spiritual happening at camp was Susan falling over a mattress and breaking her foot while trying to catch peanuts in her mouth!

In spite of all that—or maybe because of all that—Susan continued to grow, learning more and more about Jesus.

3

FRIENDLY WORDS

Susan admits that she has certain gifts in the area of building and nurturing friendships. It has always been so.

In Surabaya, Lisa Bartley was Susan's best friend. She lived just a couple of blocks away and they played together nearly every day. Lisa's father was the US consul in Surabaya.

They rode bikes, roller-skated up and down the driveway, played dress up, pretended to be Nancy Drew detectives, and made up "secret codes" for their "club."

They organized circuses in the front yard—turning cartwheels, doing backbends, being clowns.

They played *loncat tinggi* [LONE-chaht TEENG-gee]. Never heard of it? *Loncat tinggi* is a simple Indonesian game. Two people hold a long chain of rubber bands and one person runs and jumps, turning in midair to catch the rubber bands with their toes and jump over. The chain is

14

moved higher and higher until they miss, then it's the next person's turn.

At Lisa's house, they would flood their front porch that had smooth tiles, and take a running jump and slide clear across the large porch. The Bartleys also had a "monorail" where the girls would slide down a rope connected between two large trees.

Lisa and Susan used to eat *bak wan* (beef balls in a clear broth) from a street vendor. This is another newsflash for Susan's mom. Glenn says that one hard and fast rule which was deeply ingrained was never, ever drink water from the faucet. The second was like unto it: Never buy food off the street!

Lisa's family left Surabaya when Susan was in sixth grade. They kept in touch through high school. In fact, Susan wrote her during her senior year in high school and shared her testimony with her. "We lost touch after that, but I always felt compelled to pray for her," Susan confides.

Just recently Susan found Lisa's brother Hurst via the Internet and learned the sad news that Lisa died in October 1995 of unknown causes—some form of flu. She had married and had three children. She had a master's degree in psychology from Loyola University and worked with battered women. "This was heartwrenching for me to learn of her death," Susan says. "Hurst said that people loved her because she was always so kind and compassionate."

Susan also had wonderful MK friends who have remained lifetime friends. Lisa Lewis (now Gentle) and her husband, Scot, are Southern Baptist missionaries in Namibia, South Africa. Susan and Lisa have been friends for over 30 years!

Lisa said that she and Susan shared a room at Camp MiKi when they were 9, with MKs Julie Lee, Liz Applewhite, and Kerri Corwin. "I remember Susan always did have, and still has, a very gentle, quiet spirit and a sweetness in her character that always shines through," declares Lisa.

Lisa noted that they were very different: Lisa was a tomboy, boisterous type; while Susan was reticent and deeply spiritual. However, they shared a love for Camp MiKi and being Indians. The theme at camp was Native American. The MKs dressed like Indians for "powwows" and had Indian tribal names for each age-group.

According to Lisa, Susan shone in Bible Sword Drills. She knew her Bible and always had all the required verses memorized. . . . She was fast and sharp!

Lisa also remembers lots of little girl chatter about which boys at camp were cute and which ones they wished would notice them!

Another common bond was their hesitancy on Sports Day at camp. Neither girl could favorably compare her efforts with the greater physical skill of other MKs.

Many of Susan's MK friends were in Kediri, just a few hours away from Surabaya. The Kediri Baptist Hospital was there and many MKs lived there. Liz Applewhite, Nell and Mary Carpenter, and Susan had great fun playing together. Susan remembers playing games outside, roller-skating, and playing with Barbie dolls. Liz and Susan used to lip-synch the entire soundtrack of *The Sound of Music*.

Kediri meant games of "23 Skidoo," "kick the can," and "British bulldog"; and lots of fun!

But then something happened to the Ingoufs that changed Kediri from a fun place to go.

4

HEARTBREAKING WORDS IN KEDIRI

In February 1972, the doctors at the Baptist hospital in Kediri discovered that 10-year-old Ann Ingouf had cancer of the lymph system. Susan remembers her heart beating so fast as her dad told her quietly about the seriousness of her little sister's illness. The family moved to Kediri to be near the hospital.

Glenn says that when the doctors told them that Ann had only six months to live, she turned with all her heart to the Lord in fasting and prayer. In fact, the whole Mission family in Indonesia joined them as their prayer support system.

During those dark months, Glenn prayed that she would show Ann joy in the Lord even in this experience. "God surrounded me with His love as He assured me that He loved Ann more than I did and that He loved me too. I thanked Him and praised Him for this assurance.

As I prayed and cried by Ann's bed as she died, although I did not understand it, I trusted my Lord more."

Susan remembers a strange mix of memories from Kediri—the sadness of Ann's illness and her pain and the outpouring of love from people everywhere. The Frank Wells family who had served in Indonesia, now back in the States, sent Ann a card nearly every day.

On August 9, 1972, Ann was dying. Susan was very ill with a high fever. "But I knew something was happening, as the nurses and doctors came to our house and other missionaries came as well—some sitting with me. I got up to go see Ann as she lay dying. Mom was sitting on one side of her and Dad on the other. Uncle Clarence Griffin was reading Scripture. That night she went to be with the Lord.

"I couldn't sleep. Dad came in to check on me and we prayed together. I think that was when I began to really sense the comfort and friendship of the Lord. He was my Friend in a very dark hour.

"In the weeks and months that followed, the grieving was close to the surface. I remember walking into our house and suddenly realizing there was an empty place there where Ann had always been. Subconsciously I'd always assumed the presence of each member of our family in our home. Now there was a gaping hole."

The Lord knew Susan needed a special friend and He sent Kerri Corwin to visit. Susan and Kerri spent a lot of time at the Baptist hospital helping any way they could. They sat with mothers who were in labor; they watched babies being born; they watched surgery; they visited with children in the children's ward. They both thought they might be nurses someday. Kerri actually did become a nurse.

Healing came, but slowly. After the funeral the Ingoufs went as a family to the mountains to a favorite vacation spot. Susan describes spending time together crying, talking about Ann, and laughing about good memories. It was a time of renewal for the family.

Glenn tells of her struggle after Ann's death. Alone she finished packing to move from Kediri to Bandung. John was in Jakarta in a meeting. She kept coming across things of Ann's.

"I hurried to get to a Bible study I was to teach that night," Glenn recalls. "As I drove, I couldn't stop crying. I started singing a favorite song, 'O Love That Wilt Not Let Me Go.' I sang the first, then the second verse. I began the third: 'O Joy that seekest me through pain . . . I couldn't remember. I started again. Still nothing.

"I rushed home after the Bible study. Eagerly I searched the hymnal for the song. I knew that God had something to say to me:

O Joy that seekest me through pain,
I cannot close my heart to thee;
I trace the rainbow through the rain,
And feel the promise is not vain
That Morn shall tearless be.

"I sang the verse as I went to bed that night and when I woke up the next morning. John arrived home with a note from my friend Marge Worten. She wrote words of comfort quoting the third verse of 'O Love That Wilt Not Let Me Go.' God knew and He cared!"

Susan says that Ann's illness and death had a profound effect on her spiritual growth. "I found comfort in God as my Father and began to see the importance of my personal Bible study and prayer."

Ann was buried just two weeks before Susan left for boarding school in Jakarta. Susan had just turned 14.

5

WINGING WORDS IN JAKARTA

Susan took wing, packed her bags, and left home to go to Jakarta to International High School. Glenn and Susan rode the overnight train from Surabaya to Jakarta. Susan and 5 other MKs were the first to live in the Baptist hostel. Bill and Liz Corwin were the hostel parents. Their 3 children Scott, Kerri, and Kelly, were there along with Joy Beth Stuckey and Ross Fryer. The "family" grew the next year. They had 19 in the hostel, even more the following year.

"Aunt Liz and Uncle Bill were great encouragers to me," says Susan. "Aunt Liz is great fun; there's never a dull moment around her!"

Liz returns the compliment: "I believe Susan was a part of the group who helped reconstruct the carcass of our Thanksgiving turkey with transparent tape and wire and affixed it to the ceiling fan on a long string. The next morning the dorm parents (Bill and me) were greeted with a turkey carcass making lazy circles in the sky over our dining table!"

Liz declares that "Suz" became their daughter. "She is very precious to us."

Susan recalls that her hostel family encouraged her to try out for just about anything—and she didn't get into most! She tried out for cheerleading—didn't make it; girls hockey—didn't make it; musical productions—in the chorus.

Liz says that Susan was shy, but they knew she could do it. She tried out for the school's Joint Sound music group. This outstanding small group performed not only for the President of Indonesia, the President of the US, ambassadors, and their guests, but also traveled to other countries in Asia to perform. Hooray! Susan made it and sang with Joint Sound all of her high school years.

The Corwins had a dish cabinet with a glass door. Liz remembers that Susan spent hours in front of that door (her substitute mirror) perfecting her facial expressions, choreography, and singing.

Another MK friend came to Jakarta in 1974—Lisa Lewis. Already good friends, they became really close in boarding school. Lisa remembers they sat together at lunch in the center garden of the school and ate their sack lunches every day. They both sang in the choir and Joint Sound. "Susan had an incredible talent in music and drama. She had a beautiful voice!" Lisa says. "I idolized her as a great actress. She has such passion and pathos and emotion on the stage, with an ability to bring a character to life."

Lisa and Susan shared most of the same classes. Since they both loved drama, they enjoyed a special drama class with Mrs. Myerson and Mrs. Dally. Lisa laughs, "We giggled together as we got accustomed to lying on the floor for breathing exercises; we worked together as we studied improvisation, playing off each other; we rejoiced together after finishing a production we were proud of."

"I had a lot of good teachers," Susan says, "but the one who had the greatest influence on me in high school was Mrs. Ellie Heginbotham, my US literature teacher." Her husband was in Jakarta with the US State Department. Her father had been chaplain of the US Senate after Peter Marshall died.

Susan describes Ellie Heginbotham as a woman of poise and grace—elegant in her manner and demeanor. "She was a tough teacher, who challenged the socks off of me. And she was a great encourager to me. . . . To this day she continues to encourage me to use the abilities God has given me."

Liz proudly points out that Susan was always spiritually sensitive and desired very much to please the Lord. "She also knew her Bible. I remember visiting in her home in Bandung . . . and found the secret of her love for God's Word. All around the house posted on the fridge, mirrors, and above the light switches were Scriptures. . . . The Ingoufs loved, believed, and used the Word and the example of the parents became the practice of the children."

Sometime in her early teens, Susan read the biography *Bill Wallace of China*. Because of his Christian faith, he literally gave his life in a Communist prison. His sacrifice stirred in Susan a desire to follow Christ, no matter what the cost.

So Susan developed her wings academically, spiritually, and creatively. But she despaired over one area that remained dismal. Lisa Lewis Gentle said that they shared a deficit in a "dating" life. Susan confesses that she wished some boy would notice her. She wanted a boyfriend! She cried and shouted, "Why, Lord?" She felt awkward around guys she admired. She did have some good buddies she could be herself with, but that didn't count!

She recalled reading, "If you're looking for a prince—are you learning to be a princess?" So she dreamed that someday Mr. Wonderful would walk into her life. The lesson of "Do not be unequally yoked" had been taught many times, so she was very conscious of not dating a nonbeliever. She scoffed, "As if one of them would have asked me!"

Furlough time came. They spent Susan's senior year in high school in Shreveport, Louisiana. She graduated from her dad's alma mater, Byrd High School. Highland Baptist Church had a very active Acteens group and they took Susan as one of their own.

As the Ingoufs left Indonesia for furlough, Susan wrote these words:

Goodbyes
Oasis of time
   lapsed into
      forever . . .
The friendly faces
   crowded and
      suddenly
Fierce with hurt.
Gone, with the
   moving wind
      of a jet's
Takeoff.

6

FAITH WORDS AT SAMFORD UNIVERSITY

One of Susan's spiritual markers was during a revival shortly before her high school graduation. "All of a sudden I realized what it really meant to walk with the Lord—that it was a day-by-day, moment-by-moment experience. For the first time, the role of the Holy Spirit . . . became clear to me. Under His leading, I made the decision to go to Samford University in Birmingham, Alabama."

When she reached Samford, Susan was eager to grow as a Christian. She joined Shades Mountain Baptist Church and became involved in campus ministries at Samford under the leadership of Esther Burroughs. Esther's desire to grow spiritually, her gifts in communication, and her love for missions impressed Susan greatly.

Esther assures that Susan had an impact on her life as well. "Susan challenged me as her campus minister to memorize

Scripture. We met often to share with each other. My memory is that being with Susan was like being drawn into a circle of quiet, surrounded by the depth of joy and beauty in Christ that flowed from Susan to me. When she sang songs she'd written, you saw her walk with God."

During her freshman year, Stephanie Phelps mentored Susan and helped her grow spiritually. Susan recalls she was feeling overwhelmed by trying to live the Christian life. Stephanie walked into her room and Susan cried, "Stephanie, I can't witness to everybody on my hall and read my Bible every day. I can't pray for everything and everybody. I can't memorize Scripture.

"Stephanie listened to me rage on. Then she said, 'Well, it's about time you found that out—because you *can't*.' She shared 1 John 5:3. 'This is love for God: to obey his commands. And his commands are not burdensome.' She told me, 'When His commands become burdensome, somewhere along the way you've started relying on your own wisdom and strength!'

"Out of that personalized application of Scripture, I wrote a song called 'His Commands Are Not Burdensome.'

The chorus:

His commands are not burdensome,
When I'm living life by faith.
His commands are not burdensome,
Trusting in You, Lord, I obey.

Susan spent Christmas her freshman year in Shreveport, Louisiana, with her Grandmom Ingouf. It was her first Christmas away from her family. When she arrived in Shreveport about a week before Christmas, her grandmother told her that she hadn't been up to decorating. Grandfather had died earlier that year.

Susan felt terrible. She cried into her pillow that night and then it hit her. If she wanted a special Christmas, it was up to her. So she pulled out the decorations and began to make Christmas. They baked cookies; they put out the Bible opened to Luke 2. Each night they lit a candle and read part of the Christmas story and sang carols. They celebrated the birth of Jesus.

Leslie Parkman (now Roe) was Susan's roommate her sophomore year. Leslie's parents were missionaries in the Philippines. The two MKs from Southeast Asia bonded immediately. Leslie says that Susan's gentle, joyful, quiet spirit radiated her walk with God. "She never wavered in her steadfast faith. There was a deep 'settledness,' a sense of security, about Susan. This meant so much to me," Leslie claims, "as I would tend to get overcommitted in campus activities."

Leslie and Susan shared a love for music and often Susan would get out her guitar and they would sing—often songs Susan had written. One of Leslie's favorites:

It's easy to forget that the trampling
   of the grapes brings forth the wine,
And we seldom see the burdens that
   have made the person carry them so
   strong.
Father, put some pressure on me,
Give me something hard to bear,
For I know that every trial You give
   is a blessing in Your care.
So let me feel what it's like to hit
   the cold, hard ground,
So that I may know the joy of rising
   high.

Susan, however, was still shy about singing in front of others. But one day Leslie said to Susan that a church had asked her to speak and she had told them she would and Susan would come and sing. "I couldn't very easily back out then!" Susan cried. So they began speaking together and singing duets. "I slowly began to realize how much I enjoyed public speaking and sharing about the Lord's work."

When Leslie married, Susan was one of her three bridesmaids. The first Christmas after Leslie married, Susan gave her and her husband each a bookmark hand-crafted from special paper which she had painted using a special process. On each bookmark she wrote Scripture verses to encourage them in their walk with Christ. On Leslie's bookmark were these verses from Proverbs 31: "She is clothed with strength and dignity. . . . Faithful instruction is on her tongue. . . . A woman who fears the Lord is to be praised." Leslie says, "These verses are a picture of Susan."

During spring break of her sophomore year, Susan went to Oklahoma City to work with American Indians. Samford's campus ministries sponsored the trip and Esther Burroughs was the leader. Susan says that on that trip she met Cindy Walker, never realizing she would become one of her dearest friends.

Susan was part of a trio at revival services one night. They were singing "Whatever It Takes" when all of a sudden they heard a loud C-R-R-A-A-C-C-K-K and a whole pew of people was slowly sinking down! The trio dissolved into laughter while the people on the sunken pew found steadier places to sit. It was a moving experience!

Dale Milligan (now Padgett) lived on the same hall as Susan and, according to Dale, she lived more in Susan's room than her own. Then the next two years they were roommates. "We talked a lot, we supported each other, and we prayed for each other," claims Dale. "We knew when the other one had a test or was upset. Neither of us had many dates. We talked about boys, but they must not have been talking about us!"

Dale was impressed by Susan's journaling (which was begun back in Indonesia), by her understanding of God, her Scripture memorization, and her focus on God's leading and direction.

Another important memory concerned the "ice-cream escapades." Both girls loved the one-and-only perfect dessert: Baskin-Robbins ice cream!

Susan commends Dale as a great encourager in her spiritual growth. "One of the things we sometimes did as we were going to sleep at night was to say, 'Last word, His Word.' And the other would have to quote a Scripture in response."

And they left lots of notes. A sample:

Rejoice, reflect, meditate, walk,
    praise, abide in Him,
Laugh, grin, be silent, read, study,
    share!
    May His peace surround you
       His gentleness flow through you
        His joy lift you up!
        Grace,
        Susan

Dale pronounces a benediction: "I am so grateful to be called Susan's friend, to be touched by her life, to be encouraged by her notes, to have been included in her circle of influence."

The summer after Susan's junior year, she served as a summer missionary to Taiwan. "The Lord had already been working in my heart, but it was there that I faced the question of a call to missions," affirms Susan. "As I worked with Chinese children one week, I realized that this was what I wanted to give my life to—spreading the gospel in another country, among people of another language and culture."

At a national student missions conference in Nashville, Tennessee, on December 31, 1979, Susan surrendered all. "I did not put a vague name to my commitment, but wrote on my card: 'career in foreign missions.'"

In May 1980 Susan Lynn Ingouf graduated from Samford University cum laude with a bachelor of arts degree with a major in art.

Where now, Lord?

7

WORDS ON PAPER AT WOMAN'S MISSIONARY UNION

Yea! A college graduate headed for the foreign missions field! Tentative plans were already made to serve a second summer overseas—this time in Uganda in East Africa. Tim Carroll, an MK from Uganda, was taking a team—all friends. But then Susan began to sense that she was not to go. "I prayed, studied God's Word, and finally said no to the team—not fully understanding why, but feeling I must be obedient."

Then a call came from Bill O'Brien who was at the Foreign Mission Board (FMB; now International Mission Board). He asked Susan to be the FMB representative to Centrifuge at Ridgecrest that summer. Susan had never heard of the wonderful new program for teenagers, but she knew she was supposed to do it!

She worked with a great team led by Bill and Rena Henderson. She led Bible studies, missions training, teamwork—working with loads of young people.

In 1980 Susan applied at Woman's Missionary Union (WMU), Auxiliary to Southern Baptist Convention, in Birmingham, Alabama, to work as an artist. Instead, she took the position of editorial assistant for *Discovery* and *Aware,* the magazines for Girls in Action and Girls in Action leaders.

Barbara Massey is editor of *Discovery, Aware,* and *GA World* and was Susan's supervisor and friend during the over two years that Susan worked at WMU. Barbara says that Susan is a wonderful person to know and work with. "Susan is a quiet, reflective person. She was always respected by her co-workers. She was mature beyond her years. She is very organized. She is flexible.

"I also remember her genuine love for the country where she grew up—Indonesia. One evening she prepared an Indonesian meal for me. Many Indonesian objects decorated her apartment. . . . She wore Indonesian dress that evening and served a wonderful meal."

Barbara points out they shared two loves: books ("We enjoyed talking about what we were reading.") and running ("We sometimes ran together.").

"I always knew that one day Susan would be back on the missions field—not as an MK, but as a missionary herself," declares Barbara.

Susan, already a prolific writer, adds that working at WMU sharpened her editorial skills and secretarial skills. "I was also constantly reminded of my call to missions," she says, "as I read about missionaries all over the world and kept in touch with the latest news."

A precious bonus at WMU was the coming of Cindy Walker in 1981 to work there as a secretary. Cindy, also an MK, is now Cindy Gaskins, Acteens consultant for Texas WMU. Their friendship deepened as they met each day to share and pray specifically for missions.

Susan remembers that one year the Lottie Moon Christmas Offering had been behind and there was a certain goal for the number of missionaries appointed. "We prayed long and hard that both goals would be surpassed—and *rejoiced* when they were!"

Cindy received a very special gift from Susan—a beautifully bound "treasure book." The first entry in the journal is November 2, 1981. It records different segments of their shared journey after college graduation. The well-worn journal contains art, writing, memories, and quotes both love. It is truly a treasure.

A few selections:

The memo that started it all is from Susan to Cindy: "I would just love it if you and I could spent time in prayer at least once a week—maybe break time.

"I believe if we want to see specifics, we must be still enough, agree together, and ask in Jesus' name to receive specifics. I know of no other with whom I'd rather do this. What do you think?" Following the note was, as always, a Scripture: "Trust in Him at all times, O people; pour out your heart before Him" (Psalm 62:8). Also on the note, as always, was one of Susan's signature smiling faces.

An entry from Cindy sharing one of their favorite devotional books, *Come Away My Beloved*:

Muli Bwanji (Good morning)
My, my, the Lord has yet to cease His doings!

Much comfort of thought
this day.
You might enjoy (already enjoyed) page
118
in this book.

Remember your favorite part for our
"appointed time" today.
A Blessing . . .
Cindy

dear Cindy,
i am excited about our friendship!
it is a precious gift
—kindred spirits
—like minds . . .

Lots of favorite Scriptures, lots of
quotes, special lines from dearly loved
Chariots of Fire, and Cindy's favorite of all
of Susan's songs:

If I Rise

If I rise on the wings of the dawn,
If I settle on the far side of the sea—
even there Your hand will guide me,
    Your right hand hold me—
Your power will surround me in the
    night.

Here's an earthen vessel that is weak
    I cannot speak
    but can You use me anyhow?
Here's a heart that is broken
—the Lord has spoken,
    and His word demands response.

Consecrate yourselves,
   saith the Lord,
      and I will do a mighty work
        among you.
And the victory is certain
—He tears the curtain
      that divides His chosen ones.

During those years at WMU, Susan and Cindy prayed boldly for missions; and the Lord used that to deepen their faith and forge their friendship.

"Cindy continues to this day to be my lifetime friend," Susan says. "She challenges me with her heartbeat for missions and ministry."

8

SPOKEN WORDS AT SOUTHWESTERN BAPTIST THEOLOGICAL SEMINARY

Susan continued to seek and follow God's will for her life. Through her work at WMU and through experiences at her church, Shades Mountain Baptist Church in Birmingham, she began to sense the Lord's leading to go to seminary. Cindy Walker felt God's leading as well. Both resigned from WMU and entered Southwestern Baptist Theological Seminary in Fort Worth, Texas, and began classes in January 1983.

Haltom Road Baptist Church allowed Susan and Cindy to live in a missionary house their first year in seminary. Both of them joined that wonderful church.

Susan began her work on a master's degree in communications. The first semester she was in an acting class and was seeking the next step she was to take. Finally, with great unease, she wrote in her journal, "Lord, if You want me to be an actress, I'll be one." Susan sighs, "In that sentence of surrender, I knew His peace."

Doors began to open immediately. Someone had to drop out of the cast of the spring missions conference drama— the theme interpretation. The acting teacher gave them Susan's name.

Not long after, a wonderful job opened up for Susan. She became secretary and research assistant to John P. Newport, the vice-president for academic affairs at the seminary. She typed his books, thus learning computer skills. "Dr. Newport was always a great encourager to me personally and in my acting pursuits," remembers Susan.

Susan was one of the original members of the renowned drama team at Southwestern, The Company. The Company was formed by the repertory drama class during Susan's last semester as a student.

Meanwhile, some unusual happenings were going on at the missionary house at Haltom Road Baptist Church. A staff member, the minister of education and youth, Emory Gaskins, had agreed that Susan and Cindy could stay in the house. They met him their first Sunday at church. Cindy recalls that when Emory prayed that Sunday, he prayed pure Scripture. She and Susan looked at each other in amazement then looked at Emory to see if he was reading. (He was not!)

In return, Emory was expecting two "dorky" MKs. (They were not!)

In the weeks that followed, Susan and Cindy exulted in the opportunities at the church. They sang together; they did drama. They were excited over ministry and seminary and life itself.

In February, Emory asked Cindy out. By March, he knew Cindy was the one God had for him. He told her he loved her on her mother's birthday (March 17).

They were doing a Bible study one Saturday morning when God spoke to Cindy, "This is the heart you've prayed for." Cindy told Emory—and he came unglued!

Cindy had committed to do Centrifuge at Glorieta that summer (1983) and she went—with an engagement ring on her finger. On December 17, 1983, Emory and Cindy were married.

Susan wrote and sang a song especially for them:

"Behold, I do a new thing." Do you
perceive it?
Do you believe it?

Keep your eyes on the Lord
Let the Spirit be your Guide
There's assurance in God's work
for what's happening inside.

"Behold, I do a new thing." Do you
perceive it?
Do you believe it?

Come away to the place
Where your heart can hear the song.
It's a symphony of grace
—you can't help but sing along!

"Behold, I do a new thing." Do you
perceive it?
Do you believe it?

We have watched the hand of God
do what only He can do.
There's a miracle involved
in the birth of something new.

"Behold, I do a new thing." Do you
perceive it?
Do you believe it?
"Behold, I do a new thing . . ."

Susan walked through every step of this
great adventure with Cindy and rejoiced

with her. But where was that Mr. Right for her?

However, back in classes everything was going great. Susan decided to do what had never been done. Her master's thesis was a one-woman drama. She interviewed seven women from Indonesia—all Southern Baptist missionaries. Then she wrote a script about a missionary on the field.

The Scripture that imprinted itself on her mind and heart during this process was 1 Thessalonians 1:4,5 (CEV): "My dear friends, God loves you, and we know he has chosen you to be his people. When we told you the good news, it was with the power and assurance that come from the Holy Spirit, and not simply with words. You knew what kind of people we were and how we helped you." She had found her title: "Not Simply with Words."

A composite missionary emerged from the seven: Sarah. Susan said that Sarah became a living, breathing person.

The three-act presentation dealt with Sarah's call to missions (act 1), a taste of everyday life as a missionary (act 2), and Sarah's call to stay and plant her life in Indonesia (act 3).

Sarah was portrayed by Susan. But she used slides, voice-overs, and numerous sounds to enhance the performance.

Act 1 ends after numerous voices have begged Sarah to surrender to go share the gospel. At the same time, many voices have warned her to stay at home. Finally, a voice, in the sound of the wind, echoes, "Be still and know that I am God." Sarah kneels with her face turned upward. Single notes of "Wherever He Leads" play as the spotlight slowly fades.

Act 2 begins with Sarah talking to her missionary friend, Linda.

"Wait a minute, Linda. Whose idea was it to have a picnic—in the park—on a major Muslim holiday?! Where were our brains?! . . . Oh, there's nothing like a cozy picnic with the multitudes and in this heat! . . . Listen, it's times like these that I distinctly remember God's voice saying, 'Go to Switzerland and live on the ski slopes!' . . . Well, do you remember our first week in Indonesia? . . . Yes! The kids were having Burger King withdrawals, our husbands were waiting for a football game to appear on television—they're still waiting—and you and I were laid out in front of every fan we could find! . . . Oh, I thought, 'My body is never going to know energy again!' Well, as soon as Steve gets home from Jakarta, we'll get our families together and go on that picnic. . . . Oh, definitely not on a major holiday, thank you! . . . Yes. . . . Well, if he doesn't come home with

*a visa this time, this is it. We've tried every-
thing we can. . . . Thanks for praying. OK.
We'll let you know. Thanks, Linda. Bye."*

Act 3 is titled "Compelled to Stay."
Sarah remembers their coming to Indonesia and recognizing "the place" God has
for them:

*"I remember well my first impressions of
Indonesia. We arrived at night in a crowded
airport. It was raining. The electricity was off
at the guesthouse. We had no mosquito repel-
lent. But that first night I sat beside the flick-
ering flame of a kerosene lantern and wrote a
prayer of thanksgiving in my journal. I had
barely met Indonesia, but already the deep
conviction was affirmed: God had called us
here to live among these people.*

*"Today I write my thoughts and prayers
from a different perspective. This land of
uncommon beauty has become home for me.
The terraced rice fields, the palm trees, the
myriads of people are familiar sights to me
now. My ears are accustomed to the calls of
street vendors, to the sounds of roosters crow-
ing in the big city, and to the broadcast of a
Muslim call to prayer. But more than becoming familiar with this land I have grown to
love her people. It would be unspeakably hard
to leave them now."*

"Not Simply with Words" was performed many times other than its

premiere production. It also led to several years of invitations to write and perform theme interpretations at conferences across the USA.

One of Susan's Indonesian MK friends, Lisa Lewis Gentle, after many years of separation, went to Southwestern to seminary. Lisa and Susan had been compatriots in drama in Jakarta. Lisa saw Susan in "Not Simply with Words."

"I was moved to tears," she vows, "not only for the outstanding performance she gave, but I cried out of an overflow of pride to see on stage, Susan, my friend."

Susan says "Not Simply with Words" was a reminder of her own missions call. "I continued to sense that call, talk about it with others," Susan recalls. "I wondered about singleness and sought to entrust that question to the Lord. I knew that I did not feel ready to go as a single missionary. . . . I learned patience and I'm thankful for the years in which Isaiah 26:8 became precious to me: 'Yes, Lord, walking in the way of your laws, we wait for you; your name and renown are the desire of our hearts.'"

When she graduated in December 1985, Susan stayed on to work full time for John Newport and continued in drama ministry in The Company.

9

WORDS OF LOVE: TODD LAFFERTY

God is never idle! He was preparing His man for Susan! Todd Lafferty was born July 2, 1959, in Avon, Illinois; but his family moved early on to Tucson, Arizona. He grew up in a Methodist church and became a member. However, he knew something was missing from his life.

After graduating from high school, Todd played football in junior college at Arizona Western then later at the University of New Mexico. At Arizona Western he met some guys who really loved the Lord. "The more time I spent with those guys, the more I wanted what they had," Todd remembers.

So, in October 1977, 18-year-old Todd accepted Jesus Christ. "I didn't have that searching in my heart anymore!"

God began opening missions opportunities for Todd almost immediately. He went as a summer missionary to Branson, Missouri, with Campus Crusade, then as a journeyman with the Foreign Mission Board (now International Mission Board) to Aberdeen, Scotland. In 1985 he served as interim pastor of Allness Baptist Church in Aberdeen. It was there that God called Todd to foreign missions.

When he returned to the States, he served as journeyman-in-residence at two sessions of the journeyman training program. On his last day at the Missionary Learning Center in Rockville, Virginia, a friend, Cathy Wood, asked him to say hello to Susan Ingouf when he got to Southwestern Baptist Theological Seminary. Cathy told him she worked for John Newport. Todd wrote Susan's name on a piece of paper and put it in his wallet.

Todd might have forgotten that scrap of paper except that Susan's name kept coming up. A few weeks later at Missions Alive, a youth program, part of Foreign Missions Week at Glorieta, Todd was part of the personnel. He met Emory and Cindy Gaskins. They talked a lot about the new church they were starting in Fort Worth—Summerfields. They were a part of a group sent out by the mother church, Haltom Road, along with their good friend, *Susan Ingouf!*

In addition, Todd was teamed with John and Sarah Davenport that week. During one of the sessions they used a video, *Not Simply with Words*. It was inspiring and the actress was *Susan Ingouf!* She was not only committed and talented, but beautiful as well! Todd comments, "My interest level definitely rose a few notches!"

However, when Todd reached seminary, he was loaded. Studying, working at a psychiatric halfway house nearly full time, getting involved in a new church, and meeting up with old friends left him with zero time. Also, seminary remodeling had moved Susan to a temporary location.

But God pushed. Susan performed in chapel with The Company that fall.

Todd says, "Her bright eyes and radiant smile were very attractive! How could I meet her in a natural way?"

Susan's name kept popping up. Todd became friends with several members of The Company. He questioned them, but got few answers. Then one day he went to collect his Greek homework. As he walked by an office, he saw Susan's name on the desk, but she wasn't there. He decided to come back for his homework. So, on February 13, Todd walked down the hall and there she was!

They talked and then Todd "floated" off to work!

His hopes were dashed when he found out that she was seeing someone else. He didn't know it wasn't serious.

Todd began to see Susan around campus, especially in chapel. "She won't admit it, Todd confides, "but she began sitting closer and closer to where our old journeyman gang would sit!"

One day Emory Gaskins was in chapel sitting with Susan. Todd joined them. Afterwards he summoned the courage to ask her for lunch and she accepted! It was over too soon, according to Todd. As he opened the door of his truck for her, she asked him to go to an outreach at Summerfields, her church, the next Saturday.

They went and stayed to eat with Emory and Cindy. On the way home, they went for a long walk. The next day they went to each other's churches.

After only three weeks of dating, Susan dropped a bombshell. Minette Drumwright had asked her to come to work with her in the prayer office at the Foreign Mission Board. Todd's heart sunk.

Susan continued, "I told her no." "Why?" Todd asked.

"I told her I just met this guy named Todd Lafferty and I think this is a very special relationship." Susan replied. "Jerry Rankin called and asked me to come work in his office in Bangkok, Thailand, and I told him no for the same reason."

"My heart was soaring!" Todd exulted. "One morning getting ready for class—not long after this—the Lord spoke to me very clearly. 'She's the one you've been waiting for. She is not only beautiful and talented, but is mature and committed to Me. She has the world in her heart.'"

Just three weeks after Todd and Susan started dating, Todd told Susan he wanted to spend the rest of his life with her. And Susan felt the same way! They decided, however, to have an old-fashioned courtship that summer.

They met for breakfast every morning. They went to Tucson to introduce Susan to Todd's family. And Todd started planning for the day he would ask Susan to marry him.

"I decided to buy a nice journal and to take out passages from my journal concerning our story—from the time Cathy Wood mentioned her name until that day," Todd decided. "I sat and wrote 41 pages into the new journal. At the end, I wrote out my proposal. I wrapped it up and waited for 'the day.'"

Susan had a day off on August 24. They drove south to Mission Tejas State Historical Park. They ate their picnic lunch and then Todd pulled out the wrapped package. They found a bench overlooking a pond and Susan opened it. Todd read aloud from the beginning. He traced the first mention of Susan's name and how it kept popping up everywhere, and how mutual friends had encouraged their relationship.

"But most of all," Todd read, "how much I love you and how much I want to spend the rest of my life with you. You are God's best for me!"

Then he got down on one knee and asked Susan to marry him.

Susan responded by singing a song she had written in anticipation of that very day.

> It is as clear as morning sky,
> as bright as the sun—
> and I know
> that you are the one
> I'll walk through time with.
> Wherever He leads,
> I'll be by your side.
> And there's nothing I would rather
>   be
> than married to Todd Lafferty!

Yes! I love you!
Yes! I'll marry you!
Yes! I love you!
Yes!

Todd said that his butterflies lifted and his heart soared!

There was an old chapel in the park. They went in and prayed and thanked God for bringing them together.

10

WORDS OF LOVE: SUSAN INGOUF

Christmas 1986. Susan went to Birmingham, Alabama, to spend the holidays with her parents who were on furlough there. The family always shares prayer requests when they are together. Glenn, Susan's mom, put emphasis on her request for a life partner for Susan. She put five stars beside that request!

Susan had been dating a young professor at the seminary. "He was a fine person—but I just knew in my heart that we were not suited for each other," she said.

Then on February 13, 1987, a handsome, blond, blue-eyed man walked into her office—Todd Lafferty. They talked and Susan said there was an immediate recognition that he had the world in his heart.

Susan began to see Todd around campus. She was cooling down one evening after running at the recreation/aerobics center, and there he was! He walked around the track with her. The cooldown took a lot longer that night because they had so much to talk about.

One day in chapel Todd asked Susan to go to lunch. During lunch they talked about her church, Summerfields Baptist. Susan remembered they were having an Easter outreach the following Saturday, and she asked if he'd like to go. He said yes. They were both running in the Seminary Run that day, so they agreed to go after that.

That Saturday Susan laughed, "Here I am in my running shorts with my MOM (milk of magnesia) legs (they were so white!). Yet I felt perfectly at ease with him. He's interested in *me*!!! And I'm interested in *him*!!!"

Todd and Susan ended up at Emory and Cindy Gaskins's (who were encouraging the budding romance!).

On the way home, Todd asked if she'd like to walk along the river.

During the walk they decided to go to each other's churches the next day. So they went to Summerfields in the morning and to Riverside that night. They went out to dinner after church and Todd asked if she'd like to go look for bluebonnets in the countryside the next weekend. Susan said, "I was beginning to fall in love with this guy who was pursuing me!"

Bluebonnet Saturday was a beautiful day. Susan prepared a homemade version of the Ungame. They played that going along the highways and learned more about each other. They found fields of bluebonnets and took pictures of each other among them. They found Lake Whitney and spread their picnic. Todd had "Out of Africa" playing on his cassette deck. They watched the sunset before heading home.

The next week Susan sang in the seminary choir concert. Todd came and then took her to dinner. They walked on the Texas Christian University campus holding hands. Then right in front of the girls dorm, Todd kissed Susan! "I think I saw fireworks!" she claims.

Three weeks after they started dating, they had no doubts that this was for keeps. Todd told Susan he wanted to spend the rest of his life with her. Susan told him she felt the same way. They agreed on an old-fashioned courtship over the summer.

Not long after Todd and Susan began seeing each other, they were walking together on campus and saw Dr. Jack Gray. He stopped and said, "I think this is a very good idea." They felt like someone had placed a blessing on their relationship.

Todd made a cassette tape for Susan's parents. He told them about himself and his family. He gave his testimony. He also told them why he loved their daughter. Even before this, Susan's mom knew something was happening. "The way you talked about Todd in your letters was different," she said.

Two crucial matters came out as they talked. Susan had vowed she would *never* date a football player! "I had a picture in my mind that was not pretty!"

Likewise, Todd had vowed he would *never* date an actress. "They are too weird!"

In August Todd's sister, Terri, was married in Tucson. Todd invited Susan to go to meet his family. "It was thrilling to see where Todd grew up and meet those dearest to him," Susan says.

Todd's mom told Susan she knew she was special when Todd told her he had sent her flowers. He had never done that before!

August 24, 1987, was a red-letter day. Susan had the day off and they decided to drive down to Mission Tejas State Historical Park in southeast Texas. They spread their picnic under some tall pine trees. After lunch Todd brought out a package and led Susan to a bench looking out over a pond. Susan opened the package to find a journal. Todd began to read his account of their romance. Then he got down on one knee and proposed.

"We were both in tears!" Susan sighs. "Somehow I managed to sing my response to him. I'd written it some weeks before—just in case! We sat there in awe of how the Lord had led us together—and in such a short time had shown each of us that this was the life partner we'd each been praying for!"

They called their parents. There was *much* rejoicing! Todd's parents said that before Susan came along they were afraid he was going to be the first Baptist monk!

Susan's parents sent a telegram from Indonesia: "FIVE-STAR ANSWER!"

They went full-speed ahead getting ready for the wedding. Cindy Gaskins's wedding dress was a perfect fit. Susan's friend JiYoon Harris offered her a beautiful bouquet of silk flowers. A friend at church baked both the bride's and the groom's cakes as a gift. Another friend sewed the maid of honor dress for Julie.

Haltom Road had the sanctuary decorated for Christmas with pots of poinsettias.

On December 19, 1987, Emory Gaskins officiated at the wedding of Susan Ingouf and Todd Lafferty. Julie, Susan's sister, was maid of honor; and Todd's sister, Terri, was the bridesmaid. Tim, Todd's brother, was best man; and John, Susan's brother, was a groomsman. The Ingoufs were home from Indonesia for the wondrous event. Susan sang "Yes, I Love You!" to Todd.

The Laffertys spent their honeymoon in Red River, New Mexico, where it snowed on their first Christmas together!

Christmas 1986 they had never met. Christmas 1987—"Yes, I love you! Yes!!"

11

ANXIOUS WORDS,
AWAITING GOD'S PLACE

God kept revealing wonderful coinci-
dences in Susan's and Todd's lives.
Susan had signed a commitment card at a
student missions conference in Nashville,
Tennessee, on New Year's Eve 1979. On
the card she had written "career in foreign
missions." Todd has signed a commitment card stating his willingness to follow the Lord wherever He might lead. His
surrender was at a conference in Califor-
nia on New Year's Day 1980. Within a 24-
hour period—nearly a continent
apart—both headed for God's place for
them. Seven years later, they discovered it
was to go hand in hand!

After the honeymoon, it was back to
seminary for Todd, back to work for
Susan. They served as members at Summerfields Baptist Church until Todd was
called as associate pastor at Rolling Hills
Baptist Church in Weatherford, Texas.

Both Todd and Susan were involved in a student missions conference. At that time they began to take steps to be appointed international missionaries. The wall had come down in Eastern Europe and requests were flooding in. Could that be the place for them?

They reached the point in their appointment where they had to choose a place. But every time they asked the Foreign Mission Board (now International Mission Board) to put their names on a certain job description, the door would close. The job had been filled or the country decided it wasn't ready for missionaries, or an experienced missionary couple was being sent.

November 1990 was a hard month. It was on again-off again concerning Eastern Europe. Susan wrote in her journal: "You are our Father, directing our path—doing *something new*—give us eyes and hearts to *perceive* it and to glorify Your name!"

Several days later, she wrote, "I rejoice in the perfectly fitted place of service (no matter what it is). We stand waiting for Your clear path."

On November 9 Susan recorded: "Next step—to find our 'match' in country and area of service. Direct us clearly, specifically this day. . . . Give us hearts to listen and wait and follow with no reservations."

Later that same day Todd and Susan went to a meeting on Southern Asia and the Pacific. The *only* reason they went was to be with Susan's parents. Her dad was leading the session. By this time the Ingoufs were in the Foreign Mission Board (now International Mission Board) office in Richmond, Virginia. John was associate director for Southern Asia and the Pacific.

During this conference the Laffertys heard for the first time about Karachi, Pakistan. Todd poked Susan in the back when Karachi was mentioned as a top priority. Susan just grinned—like, "Sure, Karachi, Pakistan!" It had never entered their minds before!

Todd told Susan afterwards that only a converted Indiana Jones could go to Pakistan! They read the job description: Pastor of the International Church in Karachi. It felt like it "fit."

The day after discovering Karachi, the journal entry read: "Thank You that we can trust You to lead us where we should go—even as you did Abraham and Sarah. We *obey* Your command to go and *trust* You to lead us on our pilgrimage to another land, another people. Grow a love in our hearts for the specific people you've called us to."

Several days later Susan wrote: "Yesterday Spain seemed to come off our list—our hearts were one in that. Now we turn again to Pakistan and Greece. . . . We're waiting for Your clear direction."

On November 20: "Pakistan? Isaiah 61: 'anointed to preach good news to the poor' (nominal Christian culture of Pakistan); 'to bind up brokenhearted, proclaim freedom for captives' (women who feel trapped in a dual-religion marriage); 'proclaim release from darkness for the prisoners' (religious people who do not know the Lord); 'to comfort the mourning, those who grieve; to bestow beauty, gladness, praise in place of ashes, mourning, despair' (using music, art, drama?). Righteousness and praise will spring up in Pakistan before all nations—because the sovereign Lord makes it so. You give the growth!"

That same day Todd and Susan had lunch with one of the associate area directors of Southern Asia and the Pacific, Clyde Meador, and his wife, Elaine. They talked about Pakistan. Susan remembers, "We ran out of time! We were both feeling an excitement about the work there and the potential for ministry."

Nearly a week later after reading everything they could find on Pakistan: "We seem to focus on Pakistan—is that Your desire?"

November 27: "Romans 11—'Oh, the depth of the riches of Your wisdom and knowledge! How unsearchable Your judgments! Your paths beyond tracing out!' When our path seems unsearchable, we are reminded that You are the Master of the unsearchable path—we can't 'find out' the path; it must be revealed by You."

That night Todd and Susan had dinner with the Meadors and they talked a long time. "We felt ready to take the next step—toward Pakistan!"

The following night they met again with the Meadors. They affirmed, "We have a 'slow and certain' sense of God's leading us to Pakistan."

They marveled that just three weeks before they had not even *considered* Pakistan. Now they felt drawn, intrigued, excited. How appropriate that they were reading that day Romans 10:15 (NIV): "'How beautiful are the feet of those who bring good news!'"

On November 28, Todd called the Foreign Mission Board: "It's Pakistan!" In one short month the Lord led the Laffertys to His place for them.

On June 18, 1991, Todd and Susan were appointed by the Foreign Mission Board to Pakistan as career missionaries.

At the end of August they arrived in Richmond, Virginia, for seven weeks of training at the Missionary Learning Center in Rockville, Virginia.

The training was completed October 12. After a few weeks, Susan headed for Henrico Doctors Hospital in Richmond. On November 8, 1991, Rebecca Lynn Lafferty, a beautiful, blue-eyed baby girl joined the family and won their hearts!

They were praying for their visas for Pakistan by the end of the year. Then their prayer became "in a couple of months" as they moved to Bangkok, Thailand, to wait. While there, Todd assisted in student ministry at the Baptist student center.

Susan began her life as a missionaries' kid (MK) 31 years before in Bangkok as her parents waited for visas to Indonesia. Rebecca was following in her mom's footsteps.

On May 28 Clyde and Elaine Meador walked into the Laffertys' house to tell them their visas had been granted! They flew to Karachi on June 23. Uncertain words no longer! The operative word was *go!*

12

URDU WORDS IN PAKISTAN

Even before the Laffertys landed in Pakistan, they were asking for prayer that they would learn *Urdu*, the primary language of the land. Urdu, a mixture of Arabic, Persian, and Hindi is also the official language of India.

Then regularly over the next few years, the request kept coming: "Pray that we will learn to speak Urdu!"

When Todd, Susan, and Rebecca landed in Karachi, they were surrounded by the sounds of Urdu. They were also engulfed by two planeloads of Muslim pilgrims returning from their holy city, Mecca. A sea of men and boys in *shalwar kameez* (the national dress—a long tunic and baggy trousers) and a few women, completely covered, were milling around.

Welcome to Pakistan! The map on page 101 shows that Pakistan shares a border with Iran, Afghanistan, China, India, and the Arabian Sea. To the north are the Himalaya Mountains, the top of the world. Pakistan is "South Asia" with a touch of the Middle East.

Karachi is a sprawling desert town of over 16 million people. It is the commercial center of Pakistan. It is right on the Arabian Sea.

The people are from many ethnic backgrounds, from many different areas of the country. Many in the city are from other nations.

The city surprised the Laffertys: Camels and donkeys compete with buses, trucks, and cars on major thoroughfares; squatters' tents nestle next to mansions; high walls surround many homes.

They marveled at the brilliant blue skies; the Arabian sea, stormy in monsoon season, placid in the cooler time; and brilliant bougainvillea spilling over dusty walls.

As they settled in, their primary assignment during their first year was to learn Urdu. Ten hours a week Todd and Susan worked with language teachers and helpers. The rest of the time, they studied, listened to tapes, and went out to use what they had learned.

Susan learned to ask, *"Ap ka kya hal hai?"* only to have the reply, "Fine. How are you?" Many do speak English, but the Laffertys want to be able to communicate with those who do not. So they kept studying.

During the first year, on Tuesday mornings Susan and her teacher would head for the *Mangal* (Tuesday) Bazaar, under a large tent that was set up on desert sand. The bazaar had everything from fruits and vegetables to cloth and kitchenware. What an adventure! And the Urdu slowly came.

Meanwhile, Todd and Susan were immersed in the International Church of Karachi. When they began in Pakistan, the church met in the living room/dining room of a house in a residential area of the city on Fridays.

People from many different nationalities attended. On a typical Friday, a Swiss woman (worker in a leper school) might read the Scripture. Three Korean children often played violins and piano for offertory. An American woman (financial advisor for a major oil company) and a British man (executive with a major corporation) took up the offering. A man from Singapore (working with Singapore Airlines) served as church pianist. A Canadian (serving with Salvation Army) sometimes led the congregational prayer. International indeed!

Meanwhile, back at the house (which is where Susan is most of the time because women in Pakistan do stay at home) Susan is more than busy! On a typical day, Todd might go early in the morning to the vegetable/fruit *wallah* (seller). The vegetables and fruit have to be scrubbed and then soaked in a purifying solution. After drying, they are stored in the refrigerator.

Every morning Susan puts a load or two of clothes in the small Italian washing machine. Her helper, Mahesh, hangs the clothes out on the line. Mahesh also cleans the house. The constant desert sand and dust in the air requires daily sweeping and mopping.

Purified water must be used for drinking and cooking. What a chore! First, they filter the water, then boil it in huge pots. After the water finally cools, it is put in water storage containers. Now the Laffertys have a special water filter that purifies the water with a charcoal filter and ultraviolet rays. Susan exclaims, "What a blessing!" However, even with the new filter, she still does daily water chores. She fills a water thermos with ice and cold water. Then she fills the water bottles, pitchers, and ice trays with filtered water.

Susan is also busy caring for their two daughters. Rebecca was only 17 weeks old when the Laffertys left the US. In 1994, little sister Jenna joined the family.

During the day, Todd not only goes for Urdu lessons but also spends time studying for and preparing his sermon and the worship service for church. Some days he visits prisoners that the church is ministering to. Often he supervises repairs since something is always breaking down—at home and at church. He prepares for youth fellowships he leads on Sunday nights. Todd also has to spend time on paperwork and going to the police station to make sure they can stay and work in Pakistan. Add to this everyday errands— going to the market, the post office, the bank, and the moneychanger.

Electricity is sporadic, and with the temperature in the 100s in the summer and the fans not working—phew! Susan says, "I remember sitting and just praying for a breeze. Sometimes at night we lie on the tile floor near a window and try to keep cool with wet washcloths."

And they slowly but surely add Urdu words. The script is almost the same as Arabic, but with a slightly different alphabet. It is written from right to left.

During the midst of the first sweltering summer, the Laffertys went to Murree, up in the mountains, for a month of intensive language study. Susan wrote in her journal on August 19, 1992: "Thank You, Father, for this cool, clear morning. I can sit outside and see Your handiwork—the beauty of mountains and green valleys, the stately trees tall and green, the lush grass with rocks interspersed. The birds are calling to one another, the breeze lifting and bending the branches and leaves, the sound of water streaming down the side of the mountain."

Refreshed, they returned to Karachi—alas, to find one wall of their house washed away in heavy rains (unheard of in Karachi) taking with it all utilities! They lived with church members until their house was repaired.

When the Laffertys began their second year of ministry in Pakistan, they were extremely busy. Urdu lessons fell to once a week. Then Susan's second pregnancy included six months of "all-day sickness." Urdu words were few and feeble.

As the third year rolled around, Susan asked the Lord for renewed determination to learn the language. "God gave me a language tutor who was a woman and who could come to our home! Jennifer was a gift to me!" Once a week they met for two hours of conversation, reading, and writing. Susan was learning Urdu words!

13

MOTHERING WORDS FOR REBECCA AND JENNA

A November 8, 1991, event—the birth of Rebecca Lynn Lafferty—changed the whole world of Todd and Susan Lafferty. "We entered parenthood in awe of God's gift!" Susan wrote. "We learned quickly that babies do indeed change your schedule, your thinking, your *life*!"

Rebecca was not only beautiful, but also alert and content. Just a few weeks after her birth, she was sleeping through the night.

Leaving the US when Rebecca was only 17 weeks old was a challenge. Then as the Laffertys waited in Bangkok, Thailand, for their visas to be approved, Rebecca became seriously ill with viral pneumonia. Susan reflected, "During the scary first day and night, the Lord reminded us that there is another lesson of Abraham—it's about giving the Lord your all, even your child."

Susan remembers that missionaries Jerry and Elaine Perrill stood on either side of her one time when Todd had gone to take care of some business. Rebecca had had a spinal and could not be moved. Susan was holding her and weeping as Rebecca screamed. Jerry and Elaine had their hands on Susan as they prayed for her and Rebecca.

Susan gave her precious baby to the Lord and felt His peace. Rebecca's fever started falling and she fully recovered.

But babies and illnesses are natural companions. Susan wrote in her journal in August 1992: "Psalm 68—'Praise be to the Lord, to God our Savior, who daily bears our burdens!' A good word in the 'daily-ness' of Rebecca's cold/fever."

Susan has a purpose statement and the first phrase is "To have a home that is a haven of nurture and ministry."

Of course, that meant taking care of Rebecca, and later on her younger sister, Jenna. No easy task since the first year in Pakistan was mostly surviving!

Susan had some household help the first year, but she left. The second year they hired Mahesh. "Worth his weight in gold!" say the Laffertys. Susan explains that she can entrust much to him; and she can concentrate more on her family, ministry, and language study.

Being a wife to Todd and a mother to the girls is top priority. Early on, she and Todd decided not to employ an *ayah* (nurse/caregiver). They would share the responsibility of caring for Rebecca and Jenna.

In the October 1993 newsletter, the Laffertys announced the coming birth of a new baby (Jenna). The baby was due in May. Susan's doctor was Zeenat Khan at the Agha Khan University Hospital in Karachi.

The family moved into an apartment directly behind the church in 1993. By then, Becca (as she called herself) was talking up a storm. She loved to watch videos of "Barney dinosaur." Every night she'd say, "I want to read a Bible 'tory."

Susan battled six months of all-day sickness, which she soon forgot when *the* day came. On April 24, 1994, Jenna Marie Lafferty was born—a beautiful baby girl! Todd proudly announced that he witnessed the entire event and is pleased to say he didn't faint halfway through the C-section!

Susan and little Jenna had a five-day stay in the hospital and then went home to greet Grandmother Ingouf (Nani) for her monthlong visit.

Rebecca calls her little sister "my Jenna."

Todd took the customary *mitthai* (sweet candies) to several of their Pakistani friends. They wanted them to know they celebrated their new daughter's birth. In Pakistan daughters are often not valued. The Laffertys declared to all that Rebecca and Jenna are God's precious gifts to them.

In the "announcement" newsletter, Susan asked for prayer that God would give them wisdom and creativity as they raise the girls in Karachi.

In August 1994, Rebecca began preschool three times a week. An American woman taught the school in her home. During this time Jenna usually napped or played with her toys. This freed Susan to study for Bible studies and have Urdu lessons.

Being so far from the US, the girls have little contact with grandparents and extended family. But the Napiers, fellow missionaries in Karachi, are their adopted aunt and uncle. The Napier boys are their three cousins. Other missionaries who travel through Karachi often stay with the Laffertys and become adopted aunts and uncles, too.

Christmas 1994 was the family's third in Karachi. Rebecca could hardly wait for "Hannah Closet" (Santa Claus) to arrive on his camel!

Preparing for Christmas, Susan counted her blessings. Jenna, the April girl, was sitting up on her own, pulling up to stand, and scooting around the room, letting out squeals of delight. "Her grin lights up the house!" laughs her mother.

Rebecca loves going to preschool. Her classmates are French, Dutch, Peruvian, and Australian. Susan asked her to go get something for her and she replied, "I don't speak English." When asked what language she spoke, she answered, "French." Her teacher told Susan, "She's a card!"

In July 1995, the Laffertys came home for their first furlough. They lived in First Baptist Church, Irving, Texas, missionary housing so that Todd could begin working on his doctorate at Southwestern Seminary. A bout with hepatitis for Todd nearly derailed their furlough; however, he recovered in time to fly!

When they returned to Pakistan, Jenna became very ill. Her liver was enlarged and she suffered chronic diarrhea. It was determined to be caused by milk intolerance and was corrected.

In 1996 Rebecca began nursery school in the American School in Karachi. Twelve of the 14 children in her class are Pakistani Muslims. Pakistanis are very hospitable and they have afternoon tea daily. Susan has gotten to know the mothers while they wait for their children, and they often have tea with each other. Rebecca is opening doors for friendships!

The Laffertys have family fun times. They go to the playground. They go to the beach for camel rides. They have a favorite Pakistani barbecue place. They even have a Pizza Hut! It's very expensive, but for a special occasion they splurge!

They always splurge on love: love for the Father, love for each other. They pray together every night and share wonderful words from the Bible.

And Susan has some wonderful mothering words, "I am conscious that as my daughters grow up in Pakistan, they will sense the treatment of females as being inferior to men. My prayer is that they will find their worth in Christ—seeing they are chosen by Him, loved by Him—and He has a great purpose and plan for their lives."

(Note: Rebecca and Jenna will share Susan's mothering with a new little brother or sister who will join the family in May 1998.)

14

JOYFUL WORDS

Right after the New Year began in 1994, Todd performed the wedding ceremony of Ayeshah and her fiancé. Susan was present but never dreamed what a great friend Ayeshah would become.

In Susan's journal on May 15, she quoted part of Psalm 86: "Give me a sign of Your goodness, that my enemies may see it and be put to shame (v. 17)." Then she lamented, "Sometimes that's what I long for in the wilderness *years*—just a sign of Your goodness that the enemies of doubt and dryness and busyness may see it and be put to shame!"

Less than two weeks later, Todd and Susan saw the newlyweds. They invited them to come visit the International Church of Karachi—and they came the following Sunday!

Three days later, Ayeshah asked Todd about women's Bible studies. They had been canceled for the summer, but Todd told her that Susan might do a study with her. She said that she'd really like that!

Susan was elated! "Lord, is this the answer to my heartcry of May 15?"

Ayeshah and Susan started meeting every Monday evening to study the Gospel of John.

The newsletter of May 1994 recorded the first prayer request for Ayeshah.

After the first meeting, Susan wrote: "Lord, I can't judge if Ayeshah is a Christian or not. Sounds like she is a believer— though still struggling with Who Christ is. . . . I shared the bridge illustration and she seemed to agree. When I asked if she'd made a decision like that she said yes. . . . But she refers to it as 'converting to Christianity' instead of 'choosing to follow Christ.'"

At one point Susan said, "You've probably heard this." She began quoting John 3:16: "'For God so loved the world . . .'" then stopped. "Have you?"

"No." She'd never heard it. "I quoted it all, tears in my eyes. Lord, thank You for entrusting me with the privilege of giving her spiritual guidance. Give me *wisdom* in this. I pray You would teach her Who Jesus is, even this week."

June 13—the second study session. A question in the study was Have you ever "received" Jesus as your own Savior and Lord? If so, when? Susan shared her own experience of accepting Jesus.

Ayeshah answered that God had been speaking to her since childhood. Even in school she never prayed prayers written by someone else, but her own prayers to God. When she became a Catholic, she thought of Jesus as a great prophet. Then she said, "I've received Him as Savior just since we began this study!"

Susan wrote in her journal, "Thank You, Lord!! Thank You for Your work in Ayeshah's life. Thank You for her teachable heart, her desire to know You more and more!!"

The same week Ayeshah took Susan to Juma Bazaar. They were becoming really good friends.

And Susan prayed that God would guide Ayeshah's heart and her thoughts.

On July 4, Susan wrote that it was so refreshing to see how eager Ayeshah was to learn. She was also excited that Ayeshah and her husband were having a devotion and praying together every night.

On August 9, Susan wrote: "I give praise to You. . . . Just amazing to watch the miracle of growth that You work in a person's life! What joy to be a witness to it!! Father, I pray for Your hand to be on her life, guiding her with Your wisdom and understanding."

August 15. Susan met with Ayeshah. At the end of the session, Ayeshah asked, "Is there such a thing as being baptized twice?" She realized that she had not accepted Christ when she was baptized as a Catholic.

Susan rejoiced, "There You go again, Lord, teaching her so that I don't have to bring things up—she does! She wants to wait a month because she believes her husband will want to be baptized too. If he doesn't, however, she will go ahead."

Ayeshah became more excited about sharing her faith. She asked Susan for booklets and a copy of the Bridge. She faithfully reads the Scriptures, allowing God to speak to her. And Susan prays daily for her that God would make His word fresh and beautiful to her.

September 30. Baptism day! Susan wrote this prayer in her journal, "Lord, I pray that You would be glorified and honored throughout today. I pray for each one being baptized—that they would know Your presence in a special way throughout this day. I pray that Satan 'prowling around like a lion, seeking whom he may devour' would go away empty!"

Both Ayeshah and her husband were baptized and, according to Susan, glowing after the baptism! She wrote, "Thank You, Lord, for the work You're doing in their lives. . . . My heart overflows with thanksgiving for the work You're doing in Ayeshah's heart and life! You are Almighty God! Master! Tender Shepherd! Oh, Lord, bless Ayeshah and her husband with continued outpouring of Your spirit to encourage their hearts and bind them together as one in You!"

November 19. Ayeshah and her husband came over for a pancake breakfast. They shared that while they were out of the country, they were eating dinner in a restaurant and prayed before they ate. A waitress approached them later and said, "I thought I could see God in you!"

December 10. From the journal: "Father, I thank you for Ayeshah—for her partnership in the gospel from the first day until now! I am confident that You Who began a good work in her will carry it on to completion."

January 10, 1995. Ayeshah faithfully shares wherever she is. She and a group of friends were talking about someone changing and how it happens and why. Ayeshah said, "You have to search for the Truth."

One member of the group commented, "You've become a Christian."

Susan prayed that day, "Father, bless her with your *peace* and *joy*. Hold her in Your arms. . . . Do a wonderful work of strengthening her in You."

A week later, Susan wrote in her journal, "I pray for her protection. . . . Lord, hide her in the cleft of the rock. Set her on higher ground where they can only see Your glory. Protect her so she can continue being Your witness."

On February 10, this prayer of thanksgiving came from Susan: "Thank You for this growing love in my heart for this country. I think it began with Ayeshah's friendship, but slowly my eyes have opened in this past year and my heart has responded. From the beginning I *wanted* to love this place, this people; but it was not 'love at first sight.' Hopefully, it is an enduring, growing, deepening love born and nurtured by You."

May 1995. Ayeshah called Susan and told her that a co-worker saw her and she was wearing a *dupatta,* the long scarf that hangs down the back. For some time Ayeshah had been wearing a cross necklace. The co-worker said, "Oh, I see you took off your cross."

Ayeshah replied, "Oh, no, I always wear it!"

He said that he was encouraged by that because he was a Christian too. She said she hopes this can be an encouragement for all Christians.

Susan prayed, "Father, bless her abundantly with Your peace and assurance and guidance."

Ayeshah is excited about her story being told. She says, "Susan has been my mentor. Her gentle spirit, her kindness . . . but most of all, her friendship, is very special to me. We have grown closer through the years, and we have shared in each other's joys, troubles, and weaknesses. We try to encourage each other if one of us is down. Susan is such a real, down-to-earth person. No pretensions, she is just . . . Susan . . . always willing to reach out or lend a sympathetic ear. I have learned a lot from her, and she certainly is a blessing to my life.

"My faith is a growing process. . . . Through the years, tears, experiences, and joys, it means more and more to me. I clearly remember when Todd baptized me. I couldn't believe how loved I felt. But I was also aware that there was much work that the Lord was going to be doing in me! As Susan quoted to me, 'He who began a good work in you will carry it on to completion' (Phil. 1:6). I am so grateful for that promise because there are so many times when I have fallen back. . . .

It is amazing that He still loves me! He does chastise me, but I know that even at my worst, He whispers words of comfort to me, and brings me back to Him. I would be *lost* without Him, and so I know that without Him I am nothing."

15

LIVING THE WORD IN KARACHI

In June 1992, the Laffertys arrived in Karachi, Pakistan. Swallowed up in a sea of white clad men and veiled women, surrounded by the confusing sounds of a language they could not understand, choked by clouds of dust and sand, sweltering in the broiling summer sun—could this be the correct address? They wondered, "God, is this the place for us to plant our lives?"

Susan wrote:

How I searched for something
   of beauty
      wanting something to
      "anchor" my calling to this land.
No tropical garden, this
No vision of paradise
No smiling faces
   —even the music did not move easily
      into my heart.

Hard, bitter, dry, crumbling wilderness,
urban war zone
How could I ever really love
this place, this people?

Then slowly but surely, God began working a miracle. Even though Susan struggled with making their home a "haven" when the electricity was out and the house felt like a sauna, or when the water tankers couldn't deliver and they went without water for a day, she sweated and she thirsted, but she kept on.

Susan learned many lessons about the culture, like how important it is to be prepared for any guests who might come to your home. Her language tutor explained that you must serve a cup of tea without even asking your guests. "I'm growing in my understanding of what it means to be hospitable in this country," Susan explains.

Most of the hospitality extended to the Laffertys was by the tiny Mission family, Hu and Bettie Addleton and Linda Pegram. However, by 1993, the Addletons retired after 35 years of service. Linda's term ended in 1993 as well. Fortunately, the Napier family, Danny, Althea, Garrett, Cody, and Joshua arrived in August 1993.

Members of the International Church of Karachi reached out to the Laffertys. Correspondence is dotted with the following phrases: "Janice Burns's home was like a museum . . . eclectic, artsy furniture, fine art—originals. The Khokhars' simpler, bamboo furniture with western-type decor. At Janice's we were invited for 8:00 P.M. . . . Arrived and had hors d'oeuvres. . . . Dined at 9:30. At Khokhars', we went for lunch. . . . Arrived at 12:30. . . . Ate around 1:30." The friends' homes were oases in the new city.

Susan struggled with the place of women in the country. "I've been shoved, pushed, hit, overlooked in the marketplace because I am a woman," Susan grieves. It affects the way she dresses, where she travels, and how often she leaves the four walls of her house.

This incident sheds some light. One day Todd, Susan, and Rebecca were walking to the beach, a couple of blocks from where they lived then. It was a quiet day; no vehicles were on the road because a strike was going on. A motorcycle roared toward them. Susan moved behind Todd and Rebecca to let the motorcycle pass. The guy on back reached over and grabbed Susan across the chest and then they drove off laughing.

Susan had the breath knocked out of her and she was very upset. Todd was angry. As they walked home, Susan wept.

"Why are we here?" Susan cried. "The Lord spoke to me in that still small voice: 'This is what sin does. This is the darkness of evil—and you are here to be My light.'"

Part of the miracle was that Susan came to see how small her own suffering is compared to others. "I felt in some small way what many women here face on a daily basis in the marketplace and at home," she said. So her compassion for the women grew, and she kept on.

During their second year in Pakistan, Susan joined the morning Bible study at the church—"to walk among them." About that time, Janice, one of the members, asked about a Bible study in the evening. Another woman made the same request. So in the fall of 1993, a night Bible study was begun as well. At the present time there are three Bible studies. Susan still attends one morning study and teaches the night and other morning study.

During 1994, a group of women signed up to do *Experiencing God*. Ten of them met with Susan on Monday night and three on Tuesday morning. The morning group was made up of one Pakistani woman and two American women married to Pakistanis. Susan believes that out of this group came a request from the International Wives Organization (women from many countries married to Pakistanis). They needed a meeting place and are now meeting monthly in the church facilities.

A further miracle that has made Susan's heart glad is the work with the Chinese. Always Susan has loved the Chinese—growing up in Indonesia, as a summer missionary in Taiwan, as a college student in the US. In recent years an influx of Chinese in Pakistan has occurred. Some have started attending the International Church of Karachi. Most had never been to a church before. A number have come to know the Lord. Mr. Cheng was one of the first. When he was baptized, he spontaneously responded, "Jesus Christ is my Lord!" Since Mr. Cheng's step, others have come: Regina, Ren Jie, Mr. Wong, Mr. Chen, and Mr. Xie. This is the *International* Church of Karachi!

Meanwhile, Todd continues the fruitful prison ministry. Through his personal ministry and through Bible correspondence courses, lives have been changed. The church keeps growing. Over 15 countries are represented now. The church has asked permission to buy land and build. Todd takes heart and continues to "walk among the people."

Todd says, "We believe that others are being called to partner with us in this strategic Asian megacity. Could it be you?"

Susan adds, "I have seen the Lord at work in my life since we moved to Karachi. There have been some arid desert times when I have cried out for streams of refreshment. There have been some wells of deep joy as I have witnessed the Lord working in and through peoples' lives. And when I wonder why I'm here—seeing the ongoing violence; struggling when the electricity is off and it's so hot I can't think; feeling that as a woman I have little worth here—I remember my call."

So she keeps on—not simply with words, but living her faith in Pakistan.